10/18/02

Clive A. Lawton

Auschwitz

CANDLEWICK PRESS
CAMBRIDGE, MASSACHUSETTS

◀ **The entrance to Auschwitz.** The slogan "Arbeit Macht Frei" above the gates means "Work makes you free." This cynical message was erected at the entrance to many Nazi camps. Anyone passing beneath it would know that it marked the end of their freedom.

▼ **Part of the perimeter fence at Auschwitz.** It is still standing today.

The author and publishers would like to thank the Holocaust Educational Trust for their help in preparing this book.

First published in 2002 by Franklin Watts, London and Australia

First U.S. edition 2002

Library of Congress Cataloging-in-Publication Data is available.

Library of Congress Catalog Card Number 2001058115

ISBN 0-7636-1595-1

10 9 8 7 6 5 4 3 2 1

Printed in Hong Kong, China

This book was typeset in Garamond.

Candlewick Press
2067 Massachusetts Avenue
Cambridge, Massachusetts 02140

visit us at www.candlewick.com

▶ List of Auschwitz internees.
The Nazis kept detailed records of the prisoners selected for work duty.

Contents

Oświęcim

Oświęcim is a small town in the south of Poland, about 30 miles west of Krakow, on the main Krakow-Vienna railway line.

Poland has a turbulent history. Although it has existed for centuries, its neighbors have fought over it repeatedly, each claiming that it really belonged to them. However, after World War I (1914–18), these disputes appeared to be over: Poland was guaranteed independent status as a country in its own right.

Oświęcim had been little affected by outside events. Life there in the early twentieth century carried on in much the same way as it had for some 100 years. It was a quiet market town.

But, in 1939, Nazi Germany invaded Poland — and so began World War II. While most people's attention was focused on the military battles, in sleepy Oświęcim, the **Nazis** were quietly and ruthlessly carrying out the systematic murder of more than a million people. When the world discovered what they had done, this small town became better known by its German name — Auschwitz.

Today Auschwitz and the death camp the Nazis built there stand as a horrifying symbol of the worst that human beings can do. So what really happened? How did the Nazis manage to commit mass murder on such a scale? How did they justify it? These questions and more are explored in this book.

◀ **Oświęcim today.** If you stand today in the fields outside Oświęcim and look in one direction, you can see the small town in the distance. If you turn in the opposite direction, you can see the remains of the death camp that the Nazis built there. ▼

▲ **Old Oświęcim.** Before World War II, Oświęcim was an attractive little town with its fair share of fine buildings and cobbled streets.

The Nazis Invade Poland

The Nazis had planned their invasion of Poland for a long time. When they came to power in 1933, their leader Adolf Hitler made it very clear that he thought Germany had a right to take over countries in Eastern Europe to provide more land — room to live, or "Lebensraum" — for the German people.

Hitler justified his claims with his belief in the Germans' racial superiority. He never made any secret of his contempt for the Slavs: the Poles and other peoples of Eastern Europe. His racist theory argued that the German "Aryan" race deserved to be in control and that "lower" racial groups — including the Slavs — should be ordered what to do.

Although the Western Allies declared war on Germany to uphold Poland's independence, they could not stop the Nazis' efficient takeover. The invasion was so swift and Poland so poor that the Poles didn't stand a chance. They fought bravely against the terrifying power of Hitler's "Blitzkrieg" — lightning war. Blitzkrieg used aircraft to bomb enemy towns and soften up resistance before a massive advance of tanks and infantry. Poland was still using cavalry charges. Their army was quickly defeated.

The Nazis could now put their ideas into action and settle Germans in Poland. They also faced another decision: what to do about the 3.3 million Jews in Poland?

▲ **German tanks.** Since coming to power in 1933, Hitler had been experimenting with new and highly efficient systems of warfare, training a powerful fighting machine. By 1939 he was ready for war.

▲ Polish cavalry.
Many people across
Europe hoped that the
horrors of World War I
would ensure an end to
all war. As a result, few
were prepared for another
outbreak of hostilities.
What's more, countries
like Poland were largely
reliant on out-of-date
practices and weaponry.
Faced with attack by
tanks, Polish soldiers
were mounted on
horseback.

▶ Poland surrenders.
Within weeks of the
invasion and despite
courageous fighting
by the Poles,
the German army was
utterly victorious and
official Polish resistance
was swiftly crushed.

A Problem the Nazis Created

The Nazis' racist theories taught that Jews especially were to be despised. They falsely blamed Jews for all that was wrong in Europe. As soon as the Nazis took power in Germany, they instituted a series of anti-Jewish laws. Jews were restricted in the jobs they could do and where they could go.

The Nazis also persuaded the German population that "foreign" Jews didn't belong. Jews whose parents were born outside of Germany were simply "dumped" on the border. Many fled east, to Poland, which already had a large Jewish population. When Germany invaded Poland, it found itself in control of more than 3 million Jews. All, according to the Nazis, were enemies of the state.

In occupied Poland, the Nazis forced Jews to live in particular areas of the main cities — the ghettos. These were enclosed like prisons and people could leave only with a permit. The living conditions inside the ghettos were terrible — too many people crowded together without enough food. Many died.

But this was not enough for the Nazis. They wanted to wipe out the Jews altogether. Their first attempts were savage but inefficient: **S.S.** killing squads roamed the countryside, rounding up and shooting Jews, but this was not "suitable for liquidating large numbers of people in a short space of time." At the Wannsee Conference in January 1942, the Nazi leaders created plans for "a **Final Solution** to the Jewish Problem" and a policy of extermination across the whole of occupied Europe. To achieve this, they realized they would have to find the most efficient system of killing ever invented.

8

◄ **"Jews are not wanted in this place!"** Signs like this one in Schwedt in Germany were erected wherever the Nazis took power. In general, the local population went along with such visible anti-Semitism.

▲ **An early roundup.** The Nazi authorities regularly went into the ghettos and rounded up selected people for transport to the East. Usually those selected were told that they were going to labor camps.

▼ **The yellow star**, which Jews were forced to wear.

◄ **Inside the Warsaw Ghetto, 1941.** Hunger and disease were killing so many that dead bodies on the street were common.

► **The Jews of Europe.** In January 1942, Hitler's advisers met at Wannsee, near Berlin, and discussed how many Jews they would have to kill in their "**Final Solution.**" This actual list was presented, showing the number of Jews in each country, even including countries the Nazis had not yet conquered.

L a n d	Zahl
A. Altreich	131.800
Ostmark	43.700
Ostgebiete	420.000
Generalgouvernement	2.284.000
Bialystok	400.000
Protektorat Böhmen und Mähren	74.200
Estland – judenfrei –	
Lettland	3.500
Litauen	34.000
Belgien	43.000
Dänemark	5.600
Frankreich / Besetztes Gebiet	165.000
Unbesetztes Gebiet	700.000
Griechenland	69.600
Niederlande	160.800
Norwegen	1.300
B. Bulgarien	48.000
England	330.000
Finnland	2.300
Irland	4.000
Italien einschl. Sardinien	58.000
Albanien	200
Kroatien	40.000
Portugal	3.000
Rumänien einschl. Bessarabien	342.000
Schweden	8.000
Schweiz	18.000
Serbien	10.000
Slowakei	88.000
Spanien	6.000
Türkei (europ. Teil)	55.500
Ungarn	742.800
UdSSR	5.000.000
Ukraine 2.994.684	
Weißrußland aus-schl. Bialystok 446.484	
Zusammen: über	11.000.000

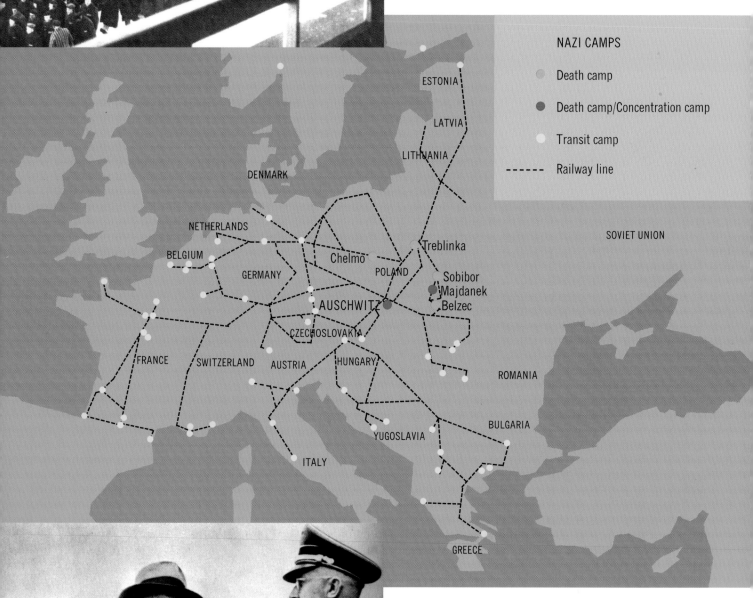

◀ **Roll call at a concentration camp.** By 1941 the Nazis had a well-established system of concentration camps. This picture was taken at Sachsenhausen camp in Germany, but similar scenes were repeated throughout occupied Europe.

▼ **Choosing the sites.** Most of the Nazi camps were located on or near the railway lines that crisscrossed Europe. The railway system itself was used by the Nazis to transport Jews and others from all over Europe to the death camps in the East. Auschwitz, on the main Krakow-Vienna line, was perfectly situated for its purpose.

NAZI CAMPS

● Death camp

● Death camp/Concentration camp

○ Transit camp

- - - - Railway line

ESTONIA
LATVIA
LITHUANIA
DENMARK
NETHERLANDS
BELGIUM
Chelmo
Treblinka
GERMANY
POLAND
Sobibor
Majdanek
Belzec
AUSCHWITZ
SOVIET UNION
CZECHOSLOVAKIA
FRANCE
SWITZERLAND
AUSTRIA
HUNGARY
ROMANIA
BULGARIA
YUGOSLAVIA
ITALY
GREECE

◀ **Himmler supervises Auschwitz's construction.**
The development of Auschwitz received attention from high-ranking Nazis. Heinrich Himmler, Hitler's second-in-command, was closely involved. He can be seen here talking to the camp architect (left); and (opposite) visiting the nearby site where a chemicals and munitions factory was being built by I.G. Farben. The plan was for camp prisoners to work in the factory. ▶

10

An Ideal Site

The Wannsee Conference may have finalized the Nazis' plans, but the preparations for a death camp at Auschwitz had already begun.

Soon after taking over Poland, the Nazis had identified an old army barracks at Auschwitz as an almost ready-made **concentration camp** — a form of prison in which large numbers could be held using very few guards. The Nazis were already using such camps in Germany to deal with their opponents. The over-crowding and poor hygiene meant that many died of malnutrition and disease.

To construct the camp, the Nazis surrounded the Auschwitz barracks with barbed wire and electrified fences, established sentry towers, and moved in a handful of guards to run it under the orders of senior Nazi officers. German convicts were employed as guards. They could be relied on to do whatever was asked in order to continue to benefit from the privilege of being freed. Within a few months the first part of Auschwitz was established as a concentration camp, mainly for Polish political prisoners.

The Nazi leaders took a keen interest in the development of Auschwitz, perhaps because they had already spotted its potential as a substantial and important camp. Auschwitz was more or less in the middle of Europe and easily accessible by rail from all over the continent. It was also some distance from major centers; no one need see what went on there.

Dusch- und Waschräume

Einer der großen Schlafsäle. An den Betten die angebrachten Eß- und Trinkgeschirre

Sanitätsstube

▲ **A camp to be proud of.**
This page from a brochure about the Oranienburg concentration camp indicates that the Nazis were not ashamed of the camps they built. They believed the harsh regime was something to boast about.

11

The Plans

Enlargement showing part of Auschwitz II.
These rows and rows of barrack huts each accommodated several hundred prisoners. ▼

Crematoria and gas chambers

Crematoria and gas chambers

THE RAMP

"LOOT" STORAGE (B-IIG)
PRISONER'S HOSPITAL (B-IIF)
GYPSY CAMP (B-IIE)
MEN'S CAMP (B-IID)
B-III SECTION
HUNGARIAN CAMP (B-IIC)
FAMILY CAMP (B-IIB)
QUARANTINE CAMP (B-IIA)
RAILCARS

▲ **Himmler inspects the plans.**
Although Auschwitz grew very quickly, its growth was carefully planned, and each development was thoroughly worked out for maximum efficiency.

▶ **The barrack huts.**
The vast majority of prisoners who entered the gates of Auschwitz-Birkenau (Auschwitz II) never saw the inside of these huts: they were killed on arrival.

That first part of the camp, known as Auschwitz I, was fairly small. Within a few months though, in the autumn of 1941, a second section of the camp was built, near the little village of Birkenau. This was sometimes called Auschwitz-Birkenau and sometimes Auschwitz II. Soon after, a third section of the camp was built—Auschwitz III.

The people imprisoned in Auschwitz I and III were mostly used as slave labor at the chemicals-munitions factory owned by I.G. Farben. Prisoners also labored in other local factories and quarries. Some had to help run the camps, too.

Originally Auschwitz II (Auschwitz-Birkenau) contained more barracks, particularly for Soviet prisoners (after the Nazi invasion of the **U.S.S.R.** in 1941), and then Jews. However, from the start, some of its inmates were simply being killed.

From 1942 onward, Jews from all over Europe were being sent there by the thousands to be killed by poisonous gas. This was originally done in an adapted farmhouse but, by 1943, special purpose-built gas chambers were installed. In 1944 the railway was extended closer to the gas chambers to speed up the killing.

▶ **The Auschwitz-Birkenau complex.**
This air reconnaisance photo taken by the Allies in 1944 shows the huge scale of Auschwitz. It had three main camps and in its few years of operation "processed" literally millions of people.

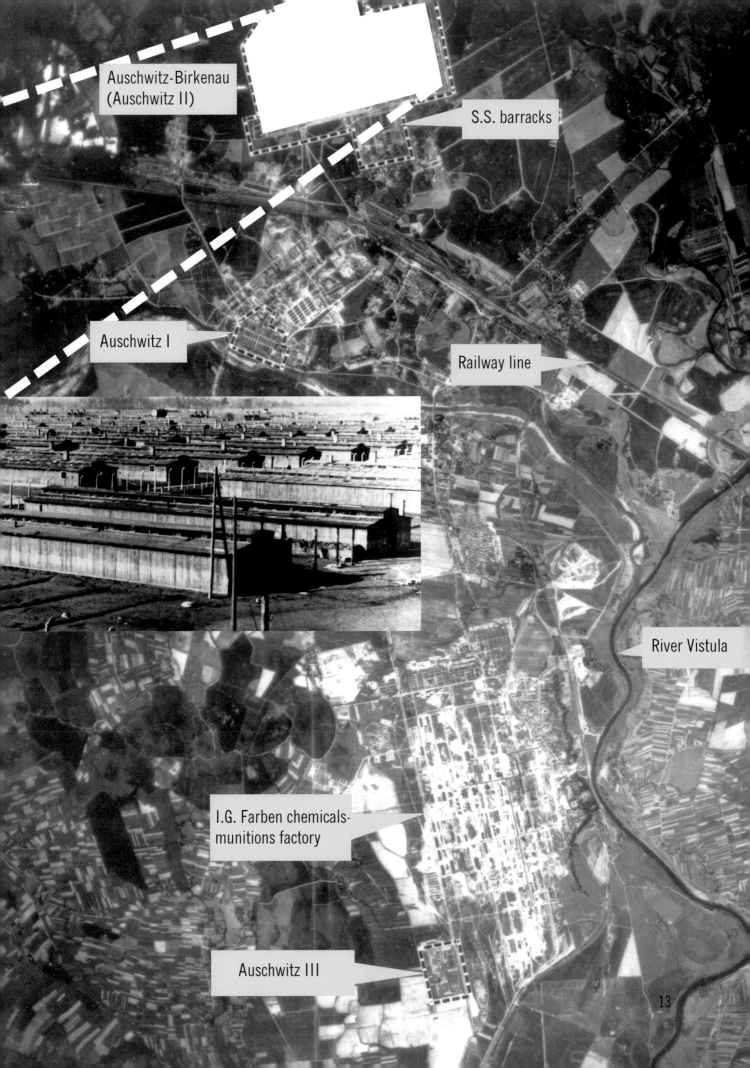

Auschwitz-Birkenau
(Auschwitz II)

S.S. barracks

Auschwitz I

Railway line

River Vistula

I.G. Farben chemicals-
munitions factory

Auschwitz III

13

66 *Every block, for instance, had a 'block elder.' They could boss you around at will, and they were the people who arranged for the collection of bread for the block from the kitchen and distributed it. The loaves were cut into four portions, and what could have been easier than to make those portions a bit undersized and keep the rest for your own purposes? That was where the camp currency came from. The camp had a highly developed hierarchy and was run almost entirely by it. To be a Kapo or a block elder meant that you belonged to the aristocracy.* 99 Anita Lasker-Wallfisch

Camp Organization

The Auschwitz camps were run as an efficient machine. Nothing was wasted. The S.S., the elite force of the Nazi regime, managed the whole process. They controlled the initial arrival of prisoners — and selected who should live and who should go straight to the **gas chambers** (the majority). They supervised those working in the camp, including ordinary soldiers, convicts from other jails, and also innocent prisoners selected for hard labor.

Many prisoners were employed in the camp itself to dispose of the dead bodies and sort the leftover possessions. Items taken from arriving prisoners were carefully stored for possible reuse: artificial limbs could be sent to the German war-wounded; shoes were valuable; even shaved hair was saved to stuff mattresses or make socks.

Prisoner-workers were controlled by fellow prisoners who took on such roles in exchange for special privileges. Jobs that gave access to medicines or food were particularly sought after. Convicts released from jail were often used to supervise prisoners on work duty. They were known as **Kapos** and were among the most ruthless "officers" in the system.

▲ **Adolf Eichmann.** A Nazi official who helped to organize the extermination of the Jews. He came to Auschwitz toward the end of the war to speed up the process.

▶ **Prisoners' possessions**. Vast quantities of goods were taken from arriving prisoners. They included jewelry, gold teeth, and other valuables, but also quite ordinary items. All were kept to be sent to Germany for reuse.

Found at Auschwitz. When the camp was liberated in 1945, piles and piles of prisoners' possessions were found there, including:

thousands of suitcases . . .

thousands of artificial limbs . . .

thousands of shoes . . .

mountains of human hair . . .

thousands of toothbrushes.

▲ **Prisoner-workers.** Prisoners selected for labor were registered in a meticulous system of record keeping. At first they were photographed; later, to save time, they were tattooed with a number. Those prisoners who were taken to the gas chambers immediately on arrival were not recorded.

15

The Transports

By the end of 1941 Auschwitz was set up to receive prisoners, mainly Jews, from all over Nazi-controlled Europe. Exploiting the excellent rail network, the Nazis ensured that Jews in many different countries were rounded up and transported there. Most often they were sent in cattle trucks or sealed freight cars, with as many as 100–150 people crammed into each one.

The first transports to arrive were from Poland and all of these Jews were immediately killed. In March 1942, transports arrived from Slovakia and France. The first transports from Holland came in July, and further transports in 1942 came mainly from Belgium, Yugoslavia, Norway, and Germany.

In 1943 transports also arrived from Greece, Italy, Latvia, and Austria, while in 1944 most arriving prisoners came from the large Jewish community in Hungary, the last to be liquidated.

Occasionally, Jews were brought from other communities, too, and many non-Jews were also sent to Auschwitz, including at least 60,000 non-Jewish Poles, 119,000 Gypsies, and 12,000 Soviet prisoners of war.

On arrival the vast majority of prisoners went straight to the gas chambers. For example, on one day, from an arrival of 1,710 deportees from Holland, 1,594 were immediately gassed, and only 116 were sent to the barracks.

▲ **In France, 1943.** French Jews were rounded up, in some cases even before the Nazi occupiers asked for them, and were sent to death camps in the East.

We were forced into line and herded into a cattle wagon, packed in like sardines. As the train progressed, it grew hotter. We could not sit down as it was too cramped, and we were all hungry. An old woman collapsed, and within minutes was dead. When at last we got out, there was a long concrete ramp leading from the station into the camp, along which streamed an endless line of people. As I got closer I realized that they were separating people into two rows. The left-hand row was full of children and old people, and I knew I must avoid that one at all costs. Arek Hersh

▼ **In Hungary, 1944.** Hungarian Jews were among the last to be rounded up. In a desperate last-minute bid, even as Germany was losing the war, Eichmann and others rushed to Hungary to speed up the transportation of Jews to Auschwitz. Hundreds of thousands were killed in the last few months of the war.

◄ **Walking to the station, Poland, 1943.** In many rural areas Jews were rounded up and marched to the nearest station to board the trains. Sometimes they had to walk for several days, carrying their suitcases with them.

▲ **Boarding the train, Poland, 1943.** Cattle and cargo trucks from all over Europe were used to transport prisoners to the death camps. Prisoners were crowded into them without food, water, or sanitation, and sent on journeys often lasting several days. Many prisoners died on the way.

17

The Selection Process

Auschwitz was never designed to accommodate all the prisoners sent there. What's more, there was no desire to keep most of the prisoners alive. In particular Auschwitz II was specifically developed to kill the maximum number of Jews as quickly as possible.

However, the Nazis recognized that it could be profitable to use some of the prisoners as slave labor for at least a period of time.

▼ **Arriving at the camp.** Prisoners emerged from the overcrowded cattle trucks onto a ramp. They were immediately hustled into a line, usually five abreast, for the selection process.

66 *When we arrived, they did not interrogate everybody, only a few. And on the basis of the replies, they pointed in two different directions. Someone dared to ask for his luggage: they replied, 'luggage afterward.' Someone else did not want to leave his wife: they said, 'together again afterward.' Mothers did not want to leave their children: they said, 'Good, good, stay with child.' They behaved calmly, like people doing normal jobs. In less than 10 minutes all the fit men had been selected. From our convoy, 96 men and 29 women entered Auschwitz I and Auschwitz III. Of the more than 500 others, not one was living two days later.* 99 Primo Levi

Therefore, as soon as the transports arrived, prisoners were made to stand in line and a selection process took place.

Those who were judged capable of hard work — on average about 20 percent of the arrivals — were told to go to the right side. The remainder — the old, the infirm, children with their mothers, and any apparently weaker people — were sent to the left and immediately taken to the gas chambers and killed.

No attempt was made to record this instantly condemned 80 percent. We can only estimate the number of people who were immediately killed by referring to the fact that so many are known to have been sent to Auschwitz who were never seen alive again. Usual estimates range from 1.5 million to 4 million people murdered at Auschwitz.

▼ **Selected for labor.** A small proportion of prisoners, mostly men but also some young women, were selected for hard labor either in the quarries or in the factories.

Making the selection. S.S. officers divided the arriving prisoners into two groups. Most women, children, and elderly people were sent to the left — for immediate progress to the "showers" (the gas chambers) and death.

19

The Cleansing Routine

Prisoners arriving at Auschwitz experienced one of two routines. Both were done in a matter-of-fact way that suggested "normality."

Those who had been chosen for the gas chambers were told that they would be going for a shower, to be deloused before rejoining their families. Their luggage was taken from them and piled on the **ramp**. They were led into a large changing room where they took off their clothes and folded them neatly for when they returned.

They were then herded into one of the gas chambers at Auschwitz II, and killed. Usually, between 2,000 and 2,500 people were gassed at a time.

Those who had been selected for hard labor or other work had their heads shaved; they were made to change out of their clothes into prison uniforms; their photographs were taken or numbers were tattooed on their forearms. They also had to hand over their luggage.

In general, when Jews were rounded up for transportation to Auschwitz, they were encouraged to think that they were going to a work camp or to be resettled in the East, and they were told to bring with them a small bag of possessions. This not only made people more cooperative but it also ensured that valuable items were brought to Auschwitz, which the Nazis could then steal.

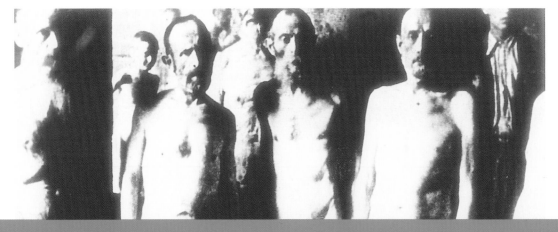

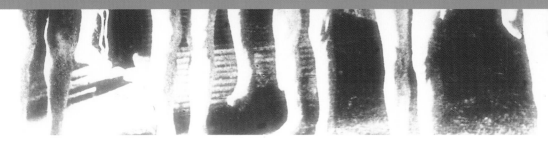

▲ **Outside the gas chambers.** Prisoners were required to strip before entering the gas chambers. They were told they were going to have a shower. This rare picture, smuggled out by a camp inmate, shows a group of prisoners waiting to enter the gas chambers.

> 66 *They tattooed me and they told us, from now on, this is your name. My name was A- 5143. Your name was your number. I felt like I was not a human person anymore. They had shaved our heads and I felt so ashamed, and also when they told us to undress, they made us feel like animals. The men were walking around and laughing and looking at us. I wanted the ground to open up and for me to be swallowed by it.* 99 Lily Malnick

▲ **Women prisoners on parade.** Those women selected to live had their hair shaved off and numbers tattooed on their arms. They spent hours standing on parade. Many women, particularly non-Jewish prisoners, worked as slave laborers in the nearby factories.

▶**Organized plunder.** One of the jobs to be done at Auschwitz was sorting through the possessions of newly arrived prisoners.

21

The Gas Chambers

As early as 1940, the Nazis had already experimented with gassing prisoners by locking them in the back of a van and redirecting the exhaust fumes into the van. Then, in September 1941, Soviet prisoners of war and others who were ill were herded down into a cellar in Auschwitz and killed there with poisonous gas. This poison gas was the fumes from prussic acid and was known under the trade name of **Zyklon B**.

Mass murders by gas started in Auschwitz II — Birkenau — at the beginning of 1942 in an adapted farmhouse. By early 1943, specially-built gas chambers disguised as showers had been built, so more Jews could be killed more quickly.

The gas chambers were tiled rooms with showerheads in the ceiling. But instead of water, poison gas was pumped in through holes in the ceiling. Once all the prisoners were dead, special teams of prisoner-workers known as the **"Sonderkommando"** dragged the bodies out and took them away for disposal.

At times prisoners arrived too fast for the gas chambers to cope with, which put the whole camp under considerable pressure. This was especially true in the last year of the war when the Nazis accelerated their transports to Auschwitz.

▶ **Waiting for death.** This group of Hungarian Jews wait to go to the gas chambers which can be glimpsed just beyond the trees. They are probably unaware of their fate.

▶ **Gas canisters.** Zyklon B was the specially developed poison gas used in the gas chambers at Auschwitz. It came in the form of pellets, which released poisonous gas when exposed to air.

❝ *They took us to a shower. They asked us to put our shoes together, tie our shoelaces together, and put our clothes down. But it turned out that the shower was really the gas. I know only that it was dark, that the Germans were terribly nervous, that when it didn't work and we came out they were very angry, shouting, 'This has never happened before!' The block elder looked at us and started to scream, 'How could it happen? Why are you back? You're not supposed to be back.' I think that was the only time in Auschwitz that the gas did not work.* ❞
Alice Lok

▼ **Russian soldiers with gas canisters.** When Auschwitz was liberated, large numbers of abandoned gas canisters were found. These Russian soldiers are posing with some of them as evidence of what had been done at Auschwitz.

23

Burning the Bodies

The thousands of prisoners who arrived at Auschwitz each day and were gassed there presented the Nazis with a further problem. It was impossible to bury the bodies quickly enough; they had to find some other method to dispose of them.

To cope with this, special **crematoria** were built at Auschwitz II with huge banks of ovens that enabled hundreds of bodies to be burned at a time.

On some occasions, however, even keeping the crematoria going at full blast could not keep pace with the mounting death toll. For this reason, some bodies were buried in large mass graves and others were disposed of in quicklime pits. (Quicklime works like a kind of acid: it reacts with the water in the human body, reducing it to dust.)

The bodies of those who had been gassed were not the only ones to be burned; every day there were also many among the camp laborers who died from overwork, malnutrition, and disease, and were disposed of in the crematoria.

Special groups of prisoners, the Sonderkommando, were forced to do the work of feeding the bodies into the ovens. Some of them buried accounts of what they had seen and what they had been made to do. The Sonderkommando also scattered human teeth around the camp to leave some evidence of the huge numbers of people killed.

24

All the crematoria were working at full blast. Last night they burned the Greek Jews [from Corfu]. The victims were kept for 27 days without food or water, first in launches, then in sealed boxcars. When they arrived at Auschwitz, the doors were unlocked, but no one got out and lined up for selection. Half of them were already dead, and the other half in a coma. The entire convoy was sent straight to number two crematorium. Later I noticed that the four lightning rods, placed on the crematorium chimneys, were twisted and bent due to the previous night's high temperatures.

From the journal of Miklos Nyiszli

◀ **Crematorium building.** One of the four specially-built brick crematoria at Auschwitz. The crematoria were kept going day and night to dispose of the remains of victims. It is estimated that, at Auschwitz, 8,000 bodies could be burned every 24 hours.

▲ **Too many bodies.** Sometimes so many people were killed in the gas chambers that the crematoria could not burn them all right away. When this happened, bodies were stacked in rows, for burial or burning at a later time.

▲ **The ovens.** Inside the crematoria were banks of ovens, each large enough to accommodate a human body. The fires were kept stoked up day and night as body after body was loaded in and turned to ashes.

▼ **Burning bodies.** This blurred photograph was one of seven smuggled out by the camp inmates themselves. It shows the Sonderkommando burning bodies out of doors because the crematoria were full to capacity.

A Living Death

A small proportion of those transported to Auschwitz were selected as being temporarily useful — to be worked to death, literally, as slave labor.

These inmates were housed in barracks in various parts of the camp. They slept in overcrowded bunks that looked more like shelves than beds. There was no proper bedding or heating, and the Polish winters were icy cold. Food rations consisted of a small amount of bread and some thin soup each day. Nowhere was there any color; the whole place seemed totally gray and lifeless.

The overcrowded conditions, the shortage of water rations, and the lack of any proper toilet or washing facilities meant that most prisoners were vulnerable to dysentery and typhoid. Becoming too weak to work was a death sentence.

Punishments were given frequently and for the slightest reason — for example, being late for roll call (prisoner inspection). Prisoners were beaten and whipped and even executed in front of the rest of the inmates. Roll call was taken frequently, often into the night. Hours and hours of standing in rows in the freezing cold took their toll, and many prisoners did not survive such treatment.

With no news from the outside world, prisoners had no idea whether there was any point in hoping for freedom or not. Suicide was not uncommon.

▲ **Inside a barrack hut at Auschwitz.** Inmates were not only stacked up on three-tiered bunks, but usually each bed was shared by several prisoners. They rarely had mattresses or blankets, there was no heating, and the Polish winters were bitterly cold.

▶ **The torture chamber.** This door led to one of the most dreaded places in Auschwitz, where prisoners were taken to betray their fellows.

▼ **Punishment.** This Russian prisoner of war was strapped in a standing position until he could stand upright no longer. Prisoners who survived such punishment were expected to work immediately after.

> *It was Yom Kippur [a Jewish fast day] and so I had eaten nothing. When I asked for a little extra in the evening, they punished me. The upper part of my body was put in an oven of the type they had there in Auschwitz II, and I was beaten on the lower part of my body, with a stick that was very thick, which they used to carry the lunch pails. At first they gave me ten strokes. I fainted; water was poured on me; then another ten blows; I fainted again — again they revived me, until I received twenty-five blows.* **"**
> Nahum Hoch

▼A suicide. For some prisoners, trying to survive became too much. Sometimes prisoners would throw themselves onto the electrified fence and end their lives.

Slave Labor

We can only estimate the number of prisoners sent to Auschwitz who went straight to the gas chambers. However, the group selected to live is well documented and there is plenty of information about their lives from the few who actually survived. Most were used for slave labor.

An early development at Auschwitz was the building of the I.G. Farben factory, which produced materials for the German war effort. It and other local factories used slave laborers. They would be marched daily from Auschwitz to the factory, and there work a 12-hour shift with few if any breaks. Most civilian workers preferred to ignore the skeletal prisoners who turned up each day.

Other prisoners worked in quarries, where injury and death were common.

Though slave labor was preferable to the other options, by 1944 conditions had deteriorated further. As German defeat loomed, the slave laborers were forced to work harder and longer, living in increasingly overcrowded conditions, and always vulnerable to disease. In Auschwitz, any prisoner not fit to work would simply be sent to the gas chamber — and everyone knew it.

❝ *They would take us outside to move huge rocks. One day we would take these huge rocks from this side and carry them to that side. The next day, they would bring us back; and we would take these same huge rocks, and carry them from that side back to this side. Now you need to know that we were undernourished. We were all weak. By the time they took us back to the barracks at night we could barely crawl. But we needed to show that we could still walk, that we were strong enough to give one more day.* **❞** Fritzie Fritshall

▼ **Women slave laborers.** These women are being marched off to their day's work in one of the nearby factories. In general, until near the end of the war, this was one of the better options at Auschwitz: factory workers received more rations and were at least indoors for much of the day.

▶ **Hard labor in a quarry.** Although this photograph was not taken at Auschwitz, but it shows the kind of work that Auschwitz prisoners carried out, breaking huge rocks into gravel and trundling the loaded gravel wagons to waiting trucks.

Guards and "Trusties"

Hard labor was not the only work done by prisoners. To reduce the number of guards required to control the camp, the S.S. used prisoners to do some of their work for them. They often appointed criminal prisoners as Kapos, who retained their few privileges by savagely applying every order to the rest of the prisoners.

Two other "trusties" roles gave protection for a short time. One was to work in the Sonderkommando. Its job was to collect and dispose of dead bodies. The Sonderkommando was regularly liquidated and a new group formed. The S.S. did not want any witnesses to survive. Some Sonderkommando members managed to thwart the S.S. by burying evidence of what they had seen. In 1944 they also staged a major sabotage attack that destroyed two of the gas chambers at Auschwitz II.

The other role was in "Canada." Canada had a reputation as a land of plenty, so it was the nickname given to the warehouse where the Nazis stored the possessions they had taken from prisoners, on arrival or after they were killed. Those who worked there — the **Canadakommando** — had to sort all this wealth. Most of them, too, were killed after a time to avoid witnesses.

▼ **Guards on watch.** The camps were run by the S.S. but many of the guards were locally recruited. Guards like these (this photo was taken at Sachsenhausen concentration camp) manned the watchtowers circling Auschwitz, ready to shoot any prisoner who stepped out of line.

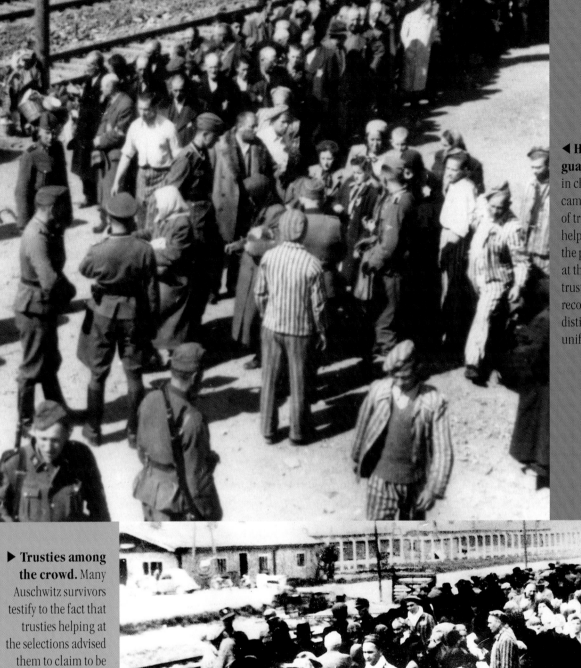

◄ Helping the guards. S.S. officers in charge of the camp used a number of trusted inmates to help them organize the prisoners arriving at the ramp. The trusties can be recognized by their distinctive striped uniform.

► Trusties among the crowd. Many Auschwitz survivors testify to the fact that trusties helping at the selections advised them to claim to be older or say they had a trade. In this tiny piece of resistance, some trusties managed to save a few lives.

❝ *To work in 'Canada' was the height of prestige because it was the source of all things valuable and useful. Canada was a paradise for 'organizing.' Enormous wealth accumulated in these few square miles. When someone knocks on your door and tells you to leave, you take whatever seems most practical: warm clothes, jewelry, and the things that are precious to you and might be of some value. So thousands, no, millions of people converged on a relatively small patch of earth carrying their most treasured possessions, and all of these were stolen.* ❞

Anita Lasker-Wallfisch

The Doctors at Auschwitz

Auschwitz was also used to conduct medical experiments. In many concentration camps, there were unscrupulous doctors who used prisoners as human guinea pigs. Jews in particular were abused in such experiments, as the Nazis felt they were "subhuman."

The most infamous S.S. doctor at Auschwitz was Dr. Josef Mengele. Nazis believed in creating a master race; so, like many Nazi scientists, Mengele was fascinated by genetics. He was convinced that conducting experiments on twins would help his research. He and his colleagues also routinely experimented with sterilizing women prisoners as part of the Nazis' plans to eradicate entire nations in this way.

If an arriving prisoner was found to be a doctor, he or she was sometimes offered the chance to work on these experiments. It was a particularly cruel choice for a doctor to face. Some agreed in the hope that they could make things better for the victims.

Experiments in Auschwitz were conducted without anesthetic or concern for the patient's survival. After undergoing such experiments, being selected to live must have had a very bitter quality.

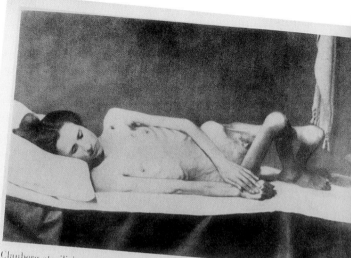

Clauberg sterilisierte Frauen ...

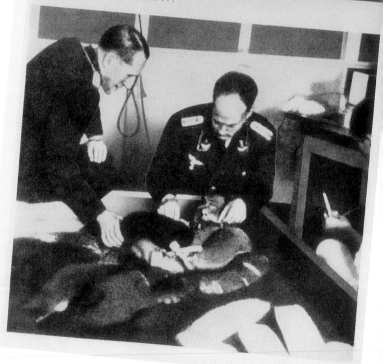

▲ **Nazi medical experiments.**
A number of doctors worked at Auschwitz, using selected prisoners as guinea pigs for their experiments. Particular attention was paid to genetic experiments on twins, and also the sterilization of women.

◀ **Entrance to the hospital block.** This is where the medical experiments were carried out. Other prisoners were also treated here if it seemed likely they might survive and provide further useful labor.

HAFTL.- KRANKENBAU
CHIRURGISCHE - ABT.
EINTRITT VERBOTEN

▶ **Dr. Josef Mengele.** Mengele presided over medical experiments on women and children. He was also credited with helping to make the gassing system at Auschwitz more scientifically effective.

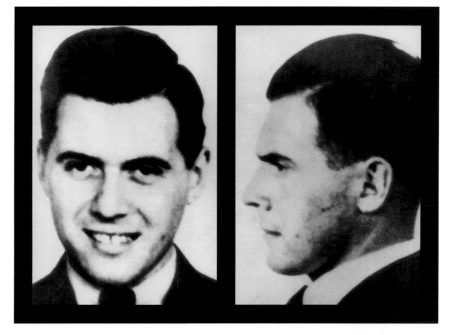

▼ **Searching for twins.** Mengele was often in attendance when new transports arrived, helping with the selection process. In particular, he was on the lookout for twins on whom he could experiment.

> ❝ *I was deported to Auschwitz in January 1943 because, while I was living in France, I insisted on wearing a Yellow Star in sympathy with the Jews. When I arrived at Auschwitz, they found I was a psychiatrist and transferred me to the medical block to carry out operations. Dr. Wirths, an S.S. doctor, wanted me to sterilize women but I refused. He was surprised that a psychiatrist would disagree with a method that he was sure would improve the race.* ❞ Dr. Adelaide Hautval

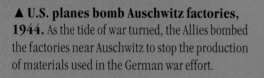

▲ U.S. planes bomb Auschwitz factories, 1944. As the tide of war turned, the Allies bombed the factories near Auschwitz to stop the production of materials used in the German war effort.

❝ *In January, Auschwitz was liquidated. They marched us out with the children's group in front. After about 10 hours walking, the children began to fall back. But whoever sat down was shot. We three boys developed a system for resting. We ran to the front and then almost stopped, until the back caught up with us. By that time we had rested, and then we ran up again and stayed warm. Suddenly, they stopped the column and told all the children that we were going to a farm. We three didn't go. The children were then taken away, and apparently shot. Only the three of us survived.* ❞

Thomas Burgenthal

The Russians Are Coming!

In 1944 American warplanes bombed the I.G. Farben factory. Many wanted the railway lines into Auschwitz to be bombed as well, to stop any more transports, but the Allies argued that this was not the best use of their resources.

Even though they faced certain defeat, the Nazis deliberately chose to speed up the killing at Auschwitz—in a last-ditch attempt to achieve their "Final Solution." Hitler's war against the Soviet Union was going particularly badly. Each side had been ruthless, and both Russian and German soldiers knew that they could expect no mercy from the other. By the end of 1944, Soviet troops had entered Poland. As the Russian army advanced, the Nazis made desperate attempts to destroy all evidence of what had been done at Auschwitz. The gas chambers were blown up, thousands of prisoners were killed, and most of the remainder were marched west toward Germany.

One of the mysteries of Auschwitz is why its commanders chose to slow their retreat by marching these prisoners across Europe. For the prisoners, already exhausted and malnourished, the forced march was another cruel twist in their ordeal. The challenge of walking hundreds of miles along icy roads, in ill-fitting clogs or without shoes at all, was too much for many of them and they died on the road.

▶ **Prisoners await liberation.** When the Nazis fled Auschwitz, they left behind some of the slave laborers and a number of children. These were the people the Russian army found when they reached the camp on January 27, 1945.

Liberation

On January 27, 1945, Soviet forces finally reached Auschwitz. They were revolted by what they found. Most people nowadays have seen pictures of the **Holocaust**, but in 1945 it was a totally new horror. A handful of half-alive prisoners were still there, but otherwise the Russians found a deserted camp with hundreds of empty barrack buildings, half-destroyed crematoria, and piles of bodies that the Nazis had not had time to bury or burn.

Immediately, the Soviet army press-ganged their German prisoners into clearing up the bodies, which had to be done at great speed because of the fear of typhus and other diseases.

Slowly, as more and more camps were liberated at the end of the war, the full scale of the Nazi atrocity became apparent. Even though rumors had circulated as early as 1942 as to what was going on in Auschwitz — and by 1943 actual reports were confirming those rumors — hardly anyone had been able to imagine the reality and scale of this industrial-style murder.

Some continued to try to cover up what had happened. The Kapos were afraid of being accused of collaborating, so they were generally not prepared to talk about what had gone on. Many of them changed their names and tried to pretend that they too had been victims.

▶ **Dead bodies frozen in the snow.** Auschwitz was evacuated so quickly that large numbers of bodies were left behind. Many inmates died in the last hours of waiting and were found lying frozen in the snow.

> *I remember opening the door of a large shed, which they called Canada. It was piled high with suitcases. There was suitcase after suitcase full of children's glasses, and I remember thinking: when the Germans murdered little children, they didn't even throw away their glasses. They kept them to use them again. And the hair: I saw all this hair, women's hair, all colors, and I wondered: how many women do you have to murder to collect that much hair?* Commander of Russian liberating forces

▼ **Clearing up.** Vast mass funerals were arranged for all the bodies found lying in and around Auschwitz. Local people and German prisoners of war were pressed into service. The locals who were questioned by Soviet officials claimed they had no idea about what had been going on at the camp.

▲ **Walking to freedom.** Many of the liberated prisoners were too weak to stand by themselves and needed the help of Russian soldiers to be able to walk out of the gates.

What Happened Next?

After the war, many survivors returned home. But most Jewish survivors could not. Their non-Jewish neighbors had frequently stood by or even helped the Nazis capture them. So many Jews were left unwanted, homeless, scattered, ill, and poor.

Special "DP" camps were set up for all the "displaced persons" who no longer had a home to go to. The victorious Allies attempted to nurse them back to normality. Generally, the victims wanted to forget what had happened to them and move on. But the experience left deep psychological scars as well as tattooed numbers on their arms.

Meanwhile, many S.S. officers and camp guards hid or fled. Twenty-one Nazi leaders were tried at Nuremberg in 1945–46 for crimes against humanity. Nearly 3,000 tons of documents, the Nazis' record of what they had done, helped to condemn most of them.

Adolf Eichmann, who masterminded the system for destroying European Jewry, had visited Auschwitz in 1944 to accelerate the killing of Hungarian Jews. He fled to South America, as did Josef Mengele. Mengele died an old man, but Eichmann was kidnapped in 1959, taken to Israel, and put on public trial. He claimed he was only following orders and had never personally murdered anybody. This was considered an inadequate defense, and he was found guilty and executed.

▲ **Eichmann on trial, 1961.** Adolf Eichmann, in a bulletproof box, stands trial in Jerusalem, Israel. His public trial, 16 years after the liberation of Auschwitz, reminded the world of the terrible atrocities that had happened there.

▶ **Children in a DP camp, 1949.**
After the war, large numbers of children needed educating in basic behavior and hygiene. These children had never used soap before.

▶ **A survivors' reunion.** These four Auschwitz survivors gathered in London in 1964. They have their arms outstretched to show their prisoner numbers tattooed on them.

▶ **The United States Holocaust Memorial Museum in Washington.** Throughout the 1980s and '90s, considerable efforts were made to record all the facts about the Holocaust before the remaining survivors died. One of the finest and most comprehensive records is to be found in the United States Holocaust Museum in Washington, D.C.

▼ **International ceremony for Auschwitz survivors.** In 1995 a multinational gathering of survivors marked the 50th anniversary of the liberation of Auschwitz. These people are determined that the world will never forget or misrepresent what happened here.

▼ **Two survivors remember.** These two Polish sisters cry as they remember their own suffering and that of their loved ones at a commemoration of the liberation of the Bergen-Belsen camp.

◀ **White Power demonstration in California, 1974.** The White Power movement adopted many Nazi ideas and symbols in its fight against racial integration.

Denial

After the war, the appalling evidence found at Auschwitz and other camps forced Nazi sympathizers to keep their opinions to themselves. As time passed, however, the shock began to fade. Old Nazi ideas started to resurface. In many cases the memory of the horror of Auschwitz and other camps could still silence them — and the capture and trial of Eichmann in 1959–61 reminded the whole world about the Holocaust.

But, by the mid 1960s, in the United States, Europe, and the Middle East, various groups were ignoring the evidence and arguing that the Jews had invented the story of the Holocaust to gain international sympathy.

Modern Nazis tried to destroy the memory of Auschwitz in people's minds. They argued that eyewitnesses were now too old to trust; that without photographs of the gas chambers in action, there was no proof of their existence; that since no one could say for sure exactly how many people had died, why believe any figures?

These people need to deny that the Holocaust happened because no decent person who knows the facts can ever again have sympathy with the ideas that the Nazis preached. Again and again, in different court cases around the world, these Holocaust deniers have been proved to be liars, their claims, false.

▶ **A neo-Nazi demonstration in Germany, 1999.** These protesters are demonstrating against immigrants being given German citizenship. There are still some people who believe that love of their own country means that they should hate all foreigners. Many of them have adopted Nazi ideas. They preach hatred against anybody who is different from them, and continue to see Jews as their fundamental enemy.

Auschwitz Today

While the Communists were in power in Poland (1945–89), they usually presented Auschwitz as a story of Polish suffering in particular. Only recently has it come to represent, more accurately perhaps, the most extreme point of the **anti-Semitism** that raged through Europe in the last century. Auschwitz itself is now facing many dilemmas.

Those who look after the site want people to visit it so that they can learn about what happened there. At the same time, however, they do not want it to become just another tourist attraction.

▲ **Tourism.** Crowds of tourists wander along one of the ramps on which a million or more prisoners awaited their fate after being unloaded from the cattle trucks.

▶ **Christian claims.** A group of Polish trade unionists erect a 6-foot-high cross in front of Auschwitz to stress the scale of Christian suffering that also happened there.

Many Christians died in Auschwitz, including Catholic priests who opposed Nazism in Poland. Although their numbers were small compared to the many Jews killed, some Catholics wish to erect large Christian memorials to them. Jews fear this would misrepresent what Auschwitz was mainly about.

Meanwhile, the people of Oświęcim want to develop their town and look forward. But each time they suggest building a nightclub or a supermarket near the remains of the death camp, the world understandably shudders at the thought of such life-celebrating activities so close to the site of such gigantic murder.

◀ **Polish nationalism.** Carrying their national flag, a group of modern Poles demonstrate in support of the construction of a supermarket near Auschwitz.

▲ **Israeli visitors.** Israelis visit Auschwitz to remember what happened before there was a Jewish state. To them, carrying an Israeli flag there is an act of defiance in the face of history.

How Do We Know?

It is important to remember that Auschwitz was not the only death camp the Nazis built. There were several others, including Belzec, Chelmo, Majdanek, Sobibor, and Treblinka, all in Poland. Auschwitz has become a symbol because it was the largest camp where the largest number of people were killed; also, because of the speed of the Russian advance, the Nazis did not have time to destroy it as they did some of the other camps.

Auschwitz was a vast complex and, between 1941 and 1945, several million people passed through it. Yet the Nazis did not advertise its existence. Photography was banned. Those prisoners who witnessed the worst of what went on were regularly killed.

Before the Nazis fled Auschwitz, they destroyed the gas chambers and most of the documentary records. They knew these were incriminating evidence. However, other sources of information have survived that reveal the extent of the horror.

The buildings

Building plans, aerial photographs, and the parts of the camp still standing enable experts to work out its scale and its processes. Although the gas chambers were blown up, experts can tell the purpose of the buildings from the position of their remains. Detailed plans exist showing how they operated. Gas chambers at other camps have survived, showing what is missing at Auschwitz.

Nazi documents and witnesses

The Nazis' ideas and their policy about the Jews are well documented. For example, full records exist of the 1942 Wannsee conference, at which plans were finalized for exterminating all the Jews of Europe, and which called for a "large killing machine in the East."

The actions of Eichmann and his subsequent testimony also provide evidence. In 1944, his role was crucial in speeding up the deportation of Hungarian Jews, even though Germany was losing the war. Why this eagerness to send them all to Auschwitz, unless it was to kill them? At his trial, Eichmann never attempted to deny that millions had been killed at Auschwitz. He merely denied that he was responsible for it.

The survivors

Some people did survive. These were mainly the prisoners used for slave labor, brought to Auschwitz from all over Europe. Their first-hand testimonies provide some of the most striking evidence, and we have quoted a few in this book.

They all knew that, if they did not keep up with the grueling demands made on them, they were destined for the gas chambers. Many tell of the continuing stench of burning bodies, especially after the arrival of each new transport.

Bodies and "loot"

Although the Nazis burned many things before they left, and also sent loads of possessions back to Germany for reuse during the war, there were still huge numbers of bodies and possessions found at Auschwitz when the camp was liberated. The abandoned loot was far in excess of the numbers of prisoners accounted for.

For example, a total of 836,255 women's coats were found. If you assume that each woman coming to Auschwitz brought one coat with her, and that there were at least as many men and probably more children arriving who would not have women's coats, you can count three million people from this discovery alone. Items like teeth were scattered all around the camp and also provide an indication of the scale of the murder.

Surviving photographs

Despite the Nazis' efforts, some photographs did survive. The Sonderkommando managed to smuggle out seven, showing prisoners getting ready for the gas chamber and bodies being sorted. (Two of them are reproduced on pages 20 and 25.) In addition, an album of some 200 photos taken at Auschwitz was found at the end of the war by a woman called Lili Jacob.

Ankunft eines Transportzuges

The Story of Lili Jacob's Album

Other than for identification purposes (for example, the photos across the center of pages 14–15), photography at Auschwitz was strictly forbidden. However, in May or June 1944, two S.S. officers — Bernard Walter, Head of the Auschwitz Identification Office, and his assistant, Ernst Hoffman — were given special permission to photograph a transport of mainly Hungarian Jews arriving from Carpatho-Ruthenia.

It is not known why Walter and Hoffman were asked to do this, but it may have been for some S.S. document that never saw the light of day. The result is an album of about 200 photographs, mainly showing the selection process on the ramp at Auschwitz and also something of what happened to these prisoners afterward.

The story of how the photographs survived is a strange one. They were pasted into an ordinary photo album which was sent to Germany. There, by a twist of fate, it was picked up at the end of the war by a prisoner, Mrs. Lili Jacob, who herself came from the region of Carpatho-Ruthenia.

In 1945 Lili Jacob was a prisoner in the Dora Nordhausen concentration camp in Germany. On May 2 she was in the camp hospital, suffering from typhus, when American soldiers arrived to liberate the camp. She and some friends were creeping to safety through the German barracks when she spotted the album. Opening it, the first thing she saw was a photo of the rabbi from her own home town. Lili Jacob fainted! Looking through the album later in the hospital, she found several photos showing members of her family, all of whom had been sent to Auschwitz and were never seen again.

Lili Jacob emigrated to the United States and took the album with her as a treasured record of her missing family. Only later did she realize its unique historical value. The album is now deposited at Yad Vashem, the Holocaust memorial in Jerusalem, Israel.

Many of the photographs used in this book come from Lili Jacob's album. Their evocative power enables us to imagine what it must have been like for the countless thousands of other prisoners arriving at the Auschwitz ramp.

Who's Who

Adolf Eichmann
Eichmann was the Supervisor of Jewish and Evacuation Affairs in the S.S. When people were not being killed quickly enough, he took charge personally. He was captured in South America in 1959, put on trial in Jerusalem, and executed in 1961.

Reinhard Heydrich
Heydrich built up the Nazi Security Service that became known as the Gestapo. His immediate boss was Heinrich Himmler. It was Heydrich who convened the Wannsee conference and oversaw the beginning of the methodical mass destruction of the Jews. He was assassinated by Czech resistance fighters in 1942.

Heinrich Himmler
Himmler was Hitler's deputy and the head of the Nazi elite force, the S.S. He took great interest in the development of Auschwitz and was the immediate boss of both Eichmann and Heydrich. He was captured at the end of the war, and committed suicide before he could be tried.

Rudolf Hoess
Hoess was a major in the S.S. and the commandant in charge of Auschwitz for most of the war. At the Wannsee conference in 1942, Hoess suggested that his camp (i.e., Auschwitz) would be a suitable place to try out the "Final Solution." He was hanged at Auschwitz in 1947.

Josef Mengele
Mengele was the most famous of the doctors working at Auschwitz. He carried out numerous experiments, on twins in particular, as well as advising on how to make the mass-murder process more efficient. He escaped to Brazil and is said to have died there of natural causes in 1979.

Glossary

Canadakommando.

Crematorium.

Gas chamber ruins.

Poison-gas canisters.

Anti-Semitism
A form of racism based on hatred of Jews.

Block elder
Someone in charge of a hut or block of prisoners in a concentration camp.

Canadakommando
Teams of Auschwitz prisoners employed to sort through the mountains of belongings that arrived with each transport of prisoners and store them in the "Canada" warehouse (so-called because Canada was considered a land of plenty).

Concentration camp
A prison system designed to contain large numbers of prisoners using the minimum number of guards. Most concentration camps had huts for the prisoners, surrounded by electrified fences and barbed wire, with towers for guards to keep watch. There are still concentration camps in some countries.

Crematorium (plural "crematoria")
A large oven designed to burn dead bodies.

"Final Solution"
A term used by the Nazis to describe the murder of all Jews: the "final solution" to what they saw as "the Jewish problem."

Gas chamber
A Nazi invention to kill large numbers of people by poison gas. The gas chambers were disguised as showers. Once they were filled with people and the doors sealed, poison gas instead of water came through holes in the ceiling.

Holocaust
Holocaust means a "massive destruction," usually by fire. The Holocaust refers to the mass destruction of millions of Jews by the Nazis in Europe during World War II.

Kapo

A prisoner who was used to supervise other prisoners on work duty. Often Kapos were convicted criminals who enjoyed their power. They were notorious for their cruelty.

Nazi

Short for National Socialist, the name of the political party founded by Hitler. Nazi ideas included the belief that countries are best ruled by an all-powerful leader, and that some groups of people, particularly Jews, deserve to be treated differently because of their race.

Ramp

The concrete platform leading from the train station into Auschwitz on which the selection process took place.

Sonderkommando

Teams of prisoners who cleared the dead bodies from the gas chambers at Auschwitz, checking them for valuables and loading them into the crematoria. *Sonder* in German means "special."

S.S.

Elite troops, originally bodyguards for the Nazi leaders. They were distinguished by their black shirts and their commitment to Nazi teachings.

U.S.S.R.

Union of Soviet Socialist Republics, a confederation of socialist/communist republics ruled from Moscow. Also known as the Soviet Union and popularly as Russia. The U.S.S.R. was disbanded in 1991.

Zyklon B

The type of poison gas used at Auschwitz. It was based on an insecticide and took the form of pellets that released poisonous prussic acid when exposed to air.

▶ From a plaque at Auschwitz.

Timeline

1933 Hitler and the Nazi party come to power in Germany.

1935 Nuremberg Laws are passed, introducing discrimination against Jews.

1938 Hitler invades Austria.

1939 Hitler invades Czechoslovakia. In September he invades Poland, and the Allies declare war. Poland is defeated; 3.3 million Polish Jews come under Nazi rule.

1940 Auschwitz I is opened as a concentration camp. Hitler invades Denmark and Norway, then Belgium and Holland, then France. Ghettos are established in Poland.

1941 Hitler invades the U.S.S.R.; 5 million Soviet Jews come under Nazi rule. Auschwitz II (Auschwitz-Birkenau) is opened. First attempts at mass killing with gas.

1942 At Wannsee, the Nazis formulate plans for a "Final Solution of the Jewish Problem." Jews from Czechoslovakia and France, Holland, Belgium, and Luxembourg are sent to Auschwitz. The news of mass killings is broadcast; no action is taken by the Allies.

1943 Gas chambers are opened at Auschwitz II. Jews from Greece, Italy, Latvia, and Austria are deported. Warsaw ghetto uprising is put down.

1944 Eichmann is put in charge of liquidating Hungarian Jews. Allied landings in Normandy and Russian advances on the Eastern Front put pressure on Germany. The number of people sent to Auschwitz increases.

1945 Auschwitz is liberated by the Russian army in January. In May the Germans surrender. Hitler commits suicide.

1946 19 Nazis are found guilty of war crimes at the Nuremberg trials.

1961 Adolf Eichmann is put to death for crimes against humanity.

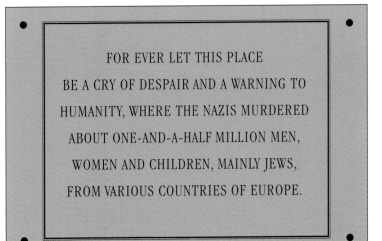

FOR EVER LET THIS PLACE
BE A CRY OF DESPAIR AND A WARNING TO
HUMANITY, WHERE THE NAZIS MURDERED
ABOUT ONE-AND-A-HALF MILLION MEN,
WOMEN AND CHILDREN, MAINLY JEWS,
FROM VARIOUS COUNTRIES OF EUROPE.

Index

Acknowledgments

Design
M&M Design Partnership

Photo research
Sue Mennell

Photographs
AKG London pp. 6t & b, 7b, 8b, 9t, 10, 11, 12, 13, 14, 14–15 (strip), 15tr-br (Michael Teller), 16–17b, 17br, 18 (inset), 20, 21t, 23t (Michael Teller), 23b, 25r, 25 (background), 26t, 31t, 34l, 36, 39b (Keith Collie), 45t, 46brb
Axiom pp. 27l (Jiri Rezac), 32b (Jiri Rezac), 43r (E. Simanor)
Franklin Watts p. 9c (courtesy of the Imperial War Museum)
Novosti, London pp. 12–13, 24, 25l, 26–27 (background), 34r, 34–35, 36–37, 37, 46trb,
©Panstwowe Muzeum Auschwitz-Birkenau pp. 3 (ref. 716/1), 5 (ref. 20 998/21)
Popperfoto pp. 2, 7t, 15t, 16–17t, 29, 30, 39t, 40t (Reuters/Reinhard Krause), 40–41 (Reuters/Peter Mueller), 41 (Reuters/Jochen Eckel), 42r (Reuters/Pawel Kopczyniski), 42–43 (Reuters/Reinhard Krause), 43l (Reuters/Pawel Kopcznski), 46tl
©Rod Shone Cover (t) and pp. 1, 2–3, 4, 4–5
Topham Picturepoint pp. 8t, 26b, 31b, 32t, 33t, 38, 39c, 42l (J. Finck), 44, 46bl
©Yad Vashem Photo Archive, Jerusalem Cover (b), endpapers and pp. 9b, 17t, 18–19, 19 (inset), 21b, 22–23, 27r, 28–29, 33b, 46tra, 46 bra

Quotations and testimonies
The author and publishers would like to thank Andrea Sonkin for her help in researching the quotations. Sources include *The Boys* by Martin Gilbert, published by Weidenfeld & Nicolson; *The World Must Know* by Michael Berenbaum, published by Little, Brown and Company; *Holocaust Journey* by Martin Gilbert, published by Phoenix; and *Inherit the Truth* by Anita Lasker-Wallfisch, published by Giles de la Mare Publishers. Other quotations are as told to the author.